The Cutting Edge of Modernity

The Cutting Edge of Modernity

Linocuts of the Grosvenor School

Gordon Samuel and Nicola Penny

Lund Humphries

First published in 2002 by

Lund Humphries
Gower House
Croft Road
Aldershot
Hampshire, GU11 3HR

and

131 Main Street
Burlington
VT 05401
USA

www.lundhumphries.co.uk

Lund Humphries is part of Ashgate Publishing

The Cutting Edge of Modernity: Linocuts of the Grosvenor School
© copyright 2002 Lund Humphries
Text © copyright 2002 Gordon Samuel and Nicola Penny
Reprinted in 2004

British Library Cataloguing-in-Publication Data
A catalogue record for this book is available from the British Library.

ISBN: 0 85331 866 2

Library of Congress Control Number: 2002103249

Designed by Chrissie Charlton and Company
Printed in China by Compass Press Ltd

Front cover illustration: Cyril Power, *Whence & Whither?* c.1930, 31 x 24 cm, 10⁴/₅ x 9¹/₂ inches
Frontispiece: Andrews and Power's studio at 2 Brook Green, Hammersmith, London, 1936

Contents

To the memory of Rex Nan Kivell (1898–1977)

Acknowledgements

A number of people have been extremely generous both with their time and expertise in the preparation of this book and we would like to thank them unreservedly for their assistance.

First and foremost Nigel Farrow of Lund Humphries and Ashgate Publishing for his constant encouragement, support and above all, interest in the linocuts. Kate Ames of Lund Humphries has also been of great help in guiding us through the pitfalls of publishing. Stephen Coppel of the Prints and Drawings Department of the British Museum is an invaluable ally and we are constantly grateful for his comprehensive research on the period and his patience in answering our questions. Recognition must also go to Mitchell Wolfson Jnr who willingly agreed to write a preface despite limitations on time.

We would also like to thank the following for their advice, assistance with photography and enthusiasm for the book:

The National Gallery of Australia
Tony Engle
Catherine Fox
Oliver Green, Head of Collections, London's Transport Museum
James Huntington-Whiteley
Mr Edmund Berry Power
Mary and Catherine Ryan — Mary Ryan Gallery, NY
Mr and Mrs Martin Squires
With the exception of figures 1–3, 10, 14–15, 20–21, 34, 39, and 41–44, all photography has been carried out by Roy Fox.

Foreword

The Grosvenor School was an early twentieth-century, cosmopolitan, 'moderne',
functional in an awareness of things-as-they-really-are aesthetic, which was both
innovative and stylish. I first encountered this pre-war predominantly British group
when the Michael Parkins Gallery organised a Grosvenor School exhibition in Milan,
Genoa, and Rome to celebrate the 100th anniversary of Marinetti's birth. And what a
pleasant surprise to find a similarly emerging new appreciation for the Italian second
Futurists, which paralleled this exhibition.

Such Italian artists as Enrico Prampolini; the group of Turin: Fillia, Diulgheroff,
and Pozzo; the Milanese: Andreoni and Munari; and the Venetians: di Bosso, Ambrosi,
and Crali, were now being re-examined in the same way as the Grosvenor crowd.
Having collected the Italian Futurists for years, I now became even more intrigued by
the similarities between the two 'forgotten' schools. Each encompassed pictorial
attitudes towards speed, movement, and perspective. Artists on both sides of the
channel were transforming the mundane into dynamic illustrations. The study of
movement and form was being extended as never before. The artists' analysis and
dissection of rushing buses, dashing crowds, and aggressive action both distorted
and simplified the image. This original visual sensation, analytical and measured,
interested me greatly.

Works from the Grosvenor School and the Italian Futurists are in the collection of
the Wolfsonian-FIU Museum and on my walls at home. I view this important art
historical initiative by Gordon Samuel and Nicola Penny with enthusiastic admiration.
I am sure that this publication on the Grosvenor School will at last foster the increased
interest that such a remarkable twentieth-century movement warrants. Hopefully this
work will lead to further comparisons and similarities being drawn between the two
schools. Here there is certainly fertile ground for scholarship.

Mitchell Wolfson Jr.
Founder of the Wolfsonian Museum, Miami Beach

The Cutting Edge of Modernity
Linocuts of the Grosvenor School

The Grosvenor School of Modern Art

The Grosvenor School of Modern Art was founded in 1925 with the aim of encouraging 'students to express their own individual ideas rather than be forced to accept worn-out academic theories'.[1] In order to provide an atmosphere that would allow pupils this personal and artistic development the founder and principal, Ian McNab (1890–1967), ensured that the school adopted a flexible approach, while offering tuition from highly respected and well-known figures within the art world. The School ran to no fixed terms and the only requirement for admission was enthusiasm rather than previous art training. Pupils were encouraged to take lessons in whichever subjects interested them. A ticketing system was employed, and a book of fifteen tickets could be purchased for one guinea and was valid for two months, allowing students to 'pick and mix' their subjects.

Prior to establishing the Grosvenor School at 33 Warwick Square, Pimlico, London, McNab had been joint principal of the Heatherley School of Fine Art and the two eventually merged in 1940. McNab was primarily known as a wood engraver and classes were offered in this discipline as well as in design, composition and life drawing. Cyril Edward Power (1872–1951), a former architect and pupil at Heatherley's was invited to become a founding lecturer, alongside the eminent critic and gallery director, Frank Rutter (1876–1973). With Power on the staff, the 1925 prospectus offered two series of ten lectures on *The Form and Structure of Buildings*, *Historical Ornament and Symbolism* and *Outline of Architectural Styles*. Power also gave twice-weekly classes on the principles of architectural sketching: *Simple Perspective for Artists* and *Elements of Architectural Ornament and Design*. Rutter's presence added more to the syllabus, providing occasional lectures on *Modern Painters from Cézanne to Picasso*. More importantly though, Rutter wrote regularly for the *Sunday Times*, providing a source of promotion for the fledgling establishment.

The progressive aims, flexible teaching and wide variety of subjects on offer are not, however, the reasons why the Grosvenor School of Modern Art is remembered today. Its present fame is due instead to Claude Flight (1881–1955), who taught the art of linocutting between 1926 and 1930. Before joining the teaching staff, Flight had already established quite an artistic reputation. He was a leading member of the Seven and Five Society before he resigned in 1928 due to Ben Nicholson's insistence on the move towards total abstraction. However, during his time as a member he was singled out for praise by the critic P. G. Konody as, 'the boldest spirit of the little coterie'.[2] He was also a founding member of the Grubb Group and The New Autumn Group, a loosely associated collection of twenty-one artists centred around St John's Wood where again he attracted critical attention: 'Mr Claude Flight is one of the most experimental members of the group and continually tries new methods of expression'.[3]

The inclusion of a subject such as linocutting on the Grosvenor School syllabus confirmed the growing interest in relief printing as a whole. Although the process of wood engraving had only been recognised as an independent technique within the previous century it had quickly flourished. John Gould Fletcher writing in *Artwork* attributed its popularity to the high degree of technical skill and hand-eye coordination that it demanded, both apparently very English qualities.[4] The 1870s saw the arrival in England of Japanese colour prints, brought over by dealers and collectors, which prompted the adoption of printing in colour from wood blocks. Despite being notoriously difficult to master, the Japanese technique bore many similarities to the methods that would be established to print from linoleum, most notably in the use of a separate block for each colour.

Linoleum was first patented in 1860 and then again three years later by the Englishman, Frederick Walton. It consisted of a mixture of cork and linseed oil that was then laid down on a canvas backing sheet, providing a tough yet pliable material, most commonly used for flooring. The discovery that it was a suitable medium for printing was made in the first decades of the twentieth century by German Expressionists such as Erich Heckel, Christian Rohlfs and Gabriele Münter and also by artists such as Wassily Kandinsky and Aleksandr Rodchenko, members of the Russian Constructivist movement. In England, Horace Brodzky and Henri Gaudier-Brzeska made the first black and white linocut prints in 1912 and 1914 respectively; Brzeska's *Wrestlers* (fig.1) remains today one of the outstanding examples of the technique. The commercial potential of the medium was also recognised early on, by the poster designer Charles Dawson, who summarised its usefulness in *The Process Engraver's Monthly*. 'This work, which I call *lino-cutting* is, after a little practice, so easy that almost any simple design can be cut double crown size in an evening.'[5]

In the years following its invention, linoleum proved itself to be a versatile material for printing, mainly due to the ease with which it could be crafted. In particular its usefulness as a means of introducing children to art was promoted by the Austrian, Professor Franz Cizek, whose exhibition of the works of his young pupils was seen by Claude Flight in 1908. This show clearly influenced Flight and he discussed Cizek's methods at length in both his books, the 1927 *Lino-Cuts: A handbook of linoleum-cut colour printing* and in 1934, *The Art and Craft of Lino Cutting and Printing*. Both books were also illustrated throughout with examples of work from both Flight's and Cizek's young pupils (fig.2). Not only might impressive results be obtained with relatively little effort but also the lino was very cheap to acquire and therefore any serious mistakes could be discarded and the artist could start again. Flight also promoted the element of fun that might be had with linocutting, again making the technique suitable for introducing art to children. 'Work in this medium appears to children as a delightful sort of game, firstly there is the expression of the child's experience in the original drawing ... then the element of sport, the digging-out the linoleum with the gouge or knife as the child digs in the sand, making little lakes, rivers, and oceans ... finally the excitement when printing and finding this new and wonderful print that has come all wet and fresh out of such an amusing process.'[6]

Although there was much obvious merit to linocutting, the medium had many detractors, and a constant battle was fought with those who believed it to be an inferior art form to the more technically demanding woodcuttir.g. Frank Morley Fletcher who was credited with introducing the Japanese technique of woodcuts to England at the turn of the century expressed his objections vociferously. He claimed that lino, 'is not suited for printing a beautiful surface of colour nor giving the finer qualities of line, and when it is used for colour the result is poor'.[7] In reply to this Flight argued that, 'greater fluency of expression is

Fig.1
Henri Gaudier–Brzeska
The Wrestlers
*c.*1914
22.5 x 27.9 cm
8$^7/_8$ x 10$^{15}/_{16}$ inches
Photograph © The British Museum

Fig.2
Alfred Schilder
The Battle of the Eagles
Cited by Flight as
'an example of a
well-filled space treated
from a naïve point of view'.

possible both in form and colour in linoleum-cut colour
printing if that printing is developed in an European way,
the technique being the means to an end instead of almost
an end in itself'.[8] Regardless of Flight's active promotion of
linocutting, it was still derided by many, the reviewer for
the *Observer* writing as late as 1934 of its 'lowly position as
the poorest of poor relations in the social register of Art'.[9]

Despite the criticism, Claude Flight's lessons in linocutting were very popular and attracted many students to the Grosvenor, including other tutors such as Cyril Power and the school secretary, Sybil Andrews (1898–1992). Flight was held in high regard by his pupils, as demonstrated by the Australian Eveline Syme (1888–1961) who discussed his tuition in 1929. 'Sometimes in his classes it is hard to remember that he is teaching, so complete is the camaraderie between him and his students. He treats them as fellow-artists rather than pupils, discusses with them and suggests to them, never dictates or enforces. At the same time he is so full of enthusiasm for his subject, and his ideas are so clear and reasoned, that it is impossible for his students not to be influenced by them.'[10]

His instructions for producing linocuts were both detailed and well recorded and in addition to many articles, he also produced two books on the subject. Both volumes stress the importance of producing work that is recognisable for what it is, a coloured print taken from cut linoleum blocks: 'A lino-cut print should not look like an oil or a water colour painting, it is a print from a soft linoleum block and so should not be taken for a wood-cut, a wood engraving, or an etching, it should take its individual place on a wall and be recognised as a lino-cut.'[11] Also of paramount importance was the composition, which Flight insisted had to be kept simple in order for the finished print to be totally effective. 'Design, or composition, is a subject of great importance, for unless the picture is well designed in the first place, all the subsequent cutting and printing will be useless, for the experience will not be expressed in a manner which is perfectly clear to the beholder.'[12] In order to aid better design, Flight promoted the abandonment of the key block, arguably his most significant contribution to the art. The key block was traditionally printed first in black or another dark colour and served to unite the entire composition by outlining objects and providing the dark masses of the work. It was undoubtedly the most important

block and one that demanded the greatest amount of detail and thought. Flight argued and taught that this technique of printing from one principal block and others of lesser importance could produce unbalanced work and instead advocated the use of blocks of equal significance. 'Two, three or four blocks of almost equal detail can be used and strength obtained where necessary by superimposing one colour over another to gain the required depth of tone.'[13] The practice of using a different piece of cut linoleum for each colour is clearly illustrated by the colour proofs from the blocks that Power used for his *Lifts*, *c*.1930 (fig.3). The colours are used to startling effect on their own, particularly the red and green that give depth to the lift shaft. The print also shows the technique of overlaying the blocks in order to provide additional tones, as demonstrated in the windows of the lift.

Flight determindly promoted the technique of linocutting as a simple process which could be easily mastered if his fastidious instructions were followed. He recommended the use of few colours, generally three or four blocks, which could be overlaid to give the impression of a more complex palette. These could be cut using basic tools, many of which could be made by the artist from household materials. In particular, he suggested the use of a large gouge fashioned from the rib of an umbrella, with 'a large bodkin filed off at the eye, and hammered into a bit of firewood'[14] as suitable for fine work. Once the blocks had been cut, Flight recommended that a trial proof be printed on tissue paper, which was less expensive than the ultra thin Japanese paper that he suggested for the edition. Choice of paper was another part of the printing process on which Flight had very definite views. Japanese and India paper were suited to the linocut process due to their transparency which let the artist see the print as it appeared through the paper. Because the paper was thin printing ink or oils sat on the surface, rather than sinking into the material, ensuring bright and long-lasting colours.

Fig.3
Cyril Power
Lifts
*c.*1930
36.6 x 23.2 cm
14³/₈ x 9¹/₈ inches
Reproduced courtesy of the
Mary Ryan Gallery, New York

Even today, almost eighty years since many of the prints were made, the colours remain vibrant and fresh. Flight also suggested other methods for adding depth of colour to works, by either first washing the paper with colour before printing or by backing the completed print with a sheet of coloured paper. As with all his ideas, he worked by example. His *Fishing in the Rain* (fig.4) *c.*1928, was one of the prints for which he used the latter technique, being mounted originally on black-brown paper. Probably his most famous use of colour washes was on the *c.*1929 *Brooklands* (fig.5) for which he experimented with the use of silver watercolour. This was brushed directly onto the paper for part of the edition and onto the grey backing sheet for the remainder.

Another factor which made linocutting a straightforward process, was that the prints were produced entirely by hand and required no mechanical press. Indeed, when selling his editions, Claude Flight promoted the personal quality of the prints, which was 'the result of the special labour that is expended on their creation'.[15] Without the press the artist simply laid the paper onto the inked block and rubbed the reverse of the sheet with the back of a spoon, another example of one of the tools that could be found around the house or studio. This technique allowed the artist greater control over the printing process as increased pressure could be applied to those areas which were intended to be darker in tone, while other areas could be left light. Both Sybil Andrews and Cyril Power made detailed notes regarding the pressure for the various areas of their linocuts, as recorded in their Print Books.[16]

Once the technique had been mastered the artist could then decide on the degree of complexity that was to be introduced into the work. Many of the artists who made the Grosvenor School famous produced highly intricate designs, fully utilising a number of different blocks and the colour combinations that they could offer (fig.33). Sybil Andrews wrote in 1986, 'the linocut print is not simple or easy. First the carving of the blocks — each in itself can be

exciting, a low-relief carving in its own right. The long careful printing, which is hard work, several times each block, all take energy and time . . . in contrast to Flight's first thought that it might be a cheap and easy way of producing prints.'[17] Cyril Power's son, Edmund, verifies Andrews' statement. He would help his father in the studio and has spoken of the effort that even a small number of prints required. The full editions were never completed at one attempt; instead the artists would print small numbers, five or ten perhaps, on demand, keeping detailed records of how much of the edition had been printed. When the Powers planned to produce linocuts they would rise early and be in the studio by at least half past eight in the morning, working constantly until ten o'clock at night or later, hardly demonstrative of the 'easy' technique Flight had suggested.

Like founders and leaders of artistic movements before him, Claude Flight had clearly defined aims for the style he promoted. He urged his students to capture the spirit of the age in which they were living, a common goal for artists of the twentieth century. He saw linocuts as the perfect medium for expressing the dynamism of a constantly changing world. 'The lino-cut is different to the other printing mediums, it has no tradition of technique behind it, so that the student can go forward without thinking of what Bewick or Rembrandt did before, he can make his own tradition, and coming at a time like the present when new ideas and ideals are shaping themselves out of apparent chaos, he can do his share in building up a new and more vital art of tomorrow.'[18] Just as Filippo Tommaso Marinetti had urged the Italian Futurists to modernise their art in order to depict the new speed of the world that had been brought about through industrialisation, Flight wanted to bring English art in line with the many technological developments his country had introduced. 'We who are accustomed to looking to the past for inspiration in our visual art accept the film and the wireless on their face values, so let us also encourage the Votaries of the linocut in this changing art world of today.'[19]

Fig.4
Claude Flight
Fishing in the Rain
*c.*1928
25.4 x 30.6 cm
10 x 12 inches

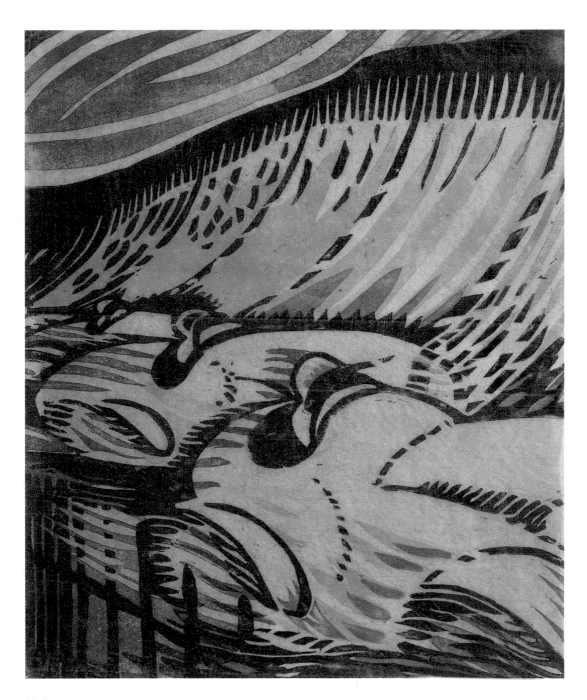

Fig.5
Claude Flight
Brooklands
*c.*1929
30.6 x 25.8 cm
12 x 10¼ inches

Despite the importance Flight placed on producing work that would bring English art in line with the Modernist forces in Europe, there is little doubt that he also had a strong social agenda to which he wanted his linocut movement to adhere. He believed passionately in the universal appeal of the prints and promoted them vigorously as a new, democratic, art form. Flight insisted that the linocuts should be produced in editions of approximately fifty to sixty prints in order to reduce the price of each print to a sum affordable to the smallest purse.[20] His vision was of a modern art, which appealed to everyone and could be found in every house. His aim for the prints was that they could be sold for the price of a beer or a cinema ticket and that they would fit into small town houses and flats. 'People live in smaller rooms, and the pictures they buy must necessarily be smaller, the price also that they are willing to pay for a picture is much less than they were willing to give formerly.'[21] Flight's utopian dream was still beyond the reach of reality. At a time when the linocuts were on sale at the Redfern Gallery for approximately three guineas the average working-class man was earning far less a week and a pint of ale could be bought for only three pence. Undaunted by this setback, Flight also recommended the establishment of a library system of lending. 'We go to libraries for our novels and our music records: let us look forward to the time when we shall have "libraries" where we can obtain prints standardized as to size to fit into our own frames in our drawing-rooms, or dining-rooms, our bedrooms and out [sic] kitchens.'[22] Realising that a system such as this required a certain degree of standardisation on the part of the artists involved, Flight included recommendations for sizing linocuts in his manuals on the technique, stating that he found eleven by nine inches the most suited for his purposes.[23] Another way of getting his art into people's houses was through the interior design company he formed with Edith Lawrence (1890–1973). Lawrence was a textile designer, a former pupil of the Slade who had exhibited at both the Royal Academy and the New English Art Club. She worked with Flight on several designs, including ideas for screens and textiles.

Claude Flight was also quick to realise that people's tastes in art required cultivation if they were to appreciate the new linocuts. While it was the duty of the artist to produce work that people could relate to by depicting the sights and sounds of the time, the general public had to be encouraged to take a fresh look at art and what to expect from it. The 1920s saw a new focus on the younger generation, who were viewed as the future for the world following the devastating losses and destruction of the First World War. In addition to this, new teaching practices were established, such as the Montessori method, encouraging self-expression and education through participation. Flight also saw the benefits of students learning his methods while still young. Linocutting taught the importance of composition and colour and could easily produce an effective result. In addition to this, Flight believed that the interest provoked would flourish and grow into a lifelong appreciation. 'Let the people but understand when they are young the possibilities of this form of art ... and their aesthetic appreciation will grow as they grow, for they will create a demand which the artists will soon supply, and perhaps a real and vital art of tomorrow, an art of the people for their homes, will arise, an art expressed, in terms of simplicity and harmony.'[24]

Fig.6
Edith Lawrence
Cricket
*c.*1930
23 x 33 cm
9 x 13 inches

The influence of Futurism can be clearly seen in the movement Flight aimed to capture in his linocuts, especially those of London as a modern city. This fascination with dynamism was eagerly noticed by critics: 'movement of all kinds interests him — passing buses, dancers, pedestrians who loom and dwindle, swings and roundabouts — all these provide him with an endless visual feast'.[27] Two of Flight's 1922 linocuts concentrate on the new feeling of speed that was prevalent in the city. *Speed* (fig.8) depicts London buses careering down Regent's Street, the surrounding pedestrians apparently blown away from their sides by the sheer velocity at which they are travelling. *Three Speeds* (fig.9) contrasts the fast-moving passengers on the buses with the queues of people who trudge down the pavement alongside.

While the Futurists occasionally appeared blinkered, concentrating solely on the depiction of universal dynamism, Flight was able to absorb influences from a wide range of movements across Europe and encouraged his students to follow suit. The impact of Cubism can be seen in the multifaceted planes that dissect the 1923 *Paris Omnibus* (fig.10). Similarly, the strong colour and decorative patterning that manifests itself in many of Flight's linocuts can be traced to the Art Deco movement of the 1920s. The 1925 *Exposition Internationale des Arts Décoratifs et Industriels Modernes* in Paris was the showcase of the new modernity in design and demonstrated how previously radical Cubist and Futurist ideas had now become commonplace. Art Deco was characterised by geometric patterns such as zigzags, chevrons and lightning, and relied on abstraction, distortion and simplification to convey its message, all of which acted as stimuli for Flight's linocuts.

In particular, Flight concentrated on producing a range of more abstract linocuts. Writing to Dorrit Black (1891–1951) in 1928 he stated, 'I believe that rather abstract ideas work better in linocuts than definite views'.[28] In order to adhere to this aim Flight evolved his own language for linocuts, which required a strict method. Once he had decided upon his subject he dissected the image into quadrants and 'golden lines' based on the proportions of the border. This resulted in a series of geometric forms that were imposed over the image, a style that often leads to complications when 'reading' the prints. Contemporary critics often mentioned the deciphering of Flight's images, so often in fact that Frank Rutter felt impelled to spring to his fellow tutor's defence in 1928. 'Every truly original painter creates a new language or at least a new dialect, the rudiments of which the spectators have to master before they can begin to understand the meaning of the message.'[29] Furthermore he continued, 'much modern painting … is frankly experimental, but without experiment there can be no discovery, without discovery there can be no progress'.[30] Certainly it can take time to understand some of Flight's linocuts. For example the critic P.G. Konody wrote of *Dirt Track Racing* (fig.11): '[T]he latest sport is represented by "Dirt-Track Racing", with crash helmets, grass plot and competitors all expressed quite clearly, to those who find the initial "clue", in Mr Flight's well known method. He subjects his forms to a treatment of radiation, enlarging or reducing them in perfect proportion as he goes along, working from the short to the long side of the frame.'[31] Not all writers were as patient, including the critic from *Apollo* magazine who reviewed the 1931 exhibition at the Redfern Gallery. 'Mr Flight's dynamic curves and disjointed curves may mean a great deal to him, but they cannot by any stretch of the term be considered "communicative", except in a very few instances, in spite of the fact that the artist has given his pictures titles which should help to put the spectator on the right track.'[32]

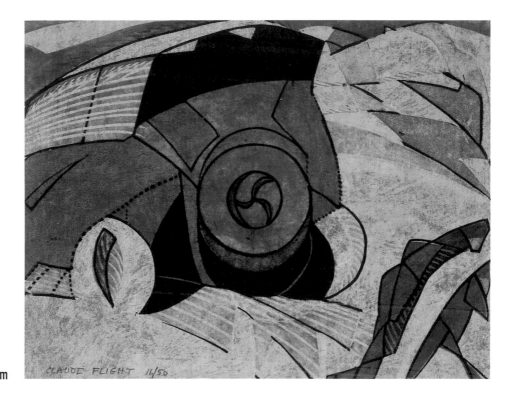

Fig.10
Claude Flight
Paris Omnibus
1923
21.8 x 28 cm
8⁵/₈ x 11 inches
Photograph
© The British Museum

Fig.11
Claude Flight
Dirt Track Racing
*c.*1928
25.6 x 30.5 cm
10 x 12 inches

Fig.12
Cyril Power
The Crypt
*c.*1928
27.3 x 18.8 cm
10³/₄ x 7¹/₂ inches

Cyril Power and Sybil Andrews

Arguably two of Flight's most successful pupils were Cyril Power and Sybil Andrews, whose skill in the medium is often deemed to have eclipsed that of their tutor. The two joined the fledgling school as part of the staff and quickly learnt the art of linocutting from Flight. Power and Andrews had first met in Bury St Edmunds where Power had encouraged Sybil Andrews to develop an interest in art that had begun with her enrolment on the John Hassall correspondence course. 'Those to whom I am most indebted would be first of all Cyril E. Power, an architect and artist. He used to sit me down (or stand) in front of the hardest building and twisting turning street we could find and say "now get on with it" and leave me to struggle correcting me after I had done the best I could on my own.'[33] Upon moving to London, Andrews joined Heatherley's, where she witnessed a 1922 lecture and demonstration of black and white woodblock printing by the Tasmanian expatriate, William Kermode, her first introduction to the possibilities of relief printing.[34]

The two artists had much in common, including from 1930 to 1938 a shared studio at 2 Brook Green, Hammersmith. On the whole they did not care for the social agenda that Flight was so eager to pursue, instead using linocuts to bring a traditional interest in subject matter up to date. Their ideas for art were outlined in an unpublished paper they produced in 1924, *Aims of the Art of To-Day*. This manifesto-style essay called on artists to steer a path between 'the art of the crude and ugly' as demonstrated by the Camden Town Group and the 'cult of sugary prettiness' which was to be found on the walls of the Royal Academy.[35] Instead, Power and Andrews wanted to produce art that reflected the contemporary world.

Fig.13
Cyril Power
The Carcase
*c.*1929
20.8 x 20 cm
8 1/4 x 7 7/8 inches

Early prints by both artists show an architectural influence, such as Power's *c.*1928 *The Crypt* (fig.12) and *The Carcase* (fig.13), which was produced the following year. The latter of these linocuts can be linked directly to the artist's previous career in architecture as it shows the incomplete extension of Lord Iveagh's library at Bradwell Manor, Essex, which Power had designed.[36] The encouragement the older artist offered to Sybil Andrews can be seen in two prints dating from 1929, *Concert Hall* (fig.14) and *Theatre* (fig.15), both of which give precedence to the structure of buildings rather than the people who occupy them. It was not long however before both artists were taking up Claude Flight's battlecry and producing work that depicted the modern city in all its glory. 'This speeding up of life in general ... is one of the interesting and psychologically important features of to-day. ... Traffic problems, transport problems; everybody is on the rush either for work or pleasure. ... The Painter cannot but be influenced by the restlessness of his surroundings.'[37]

Perhaps the most dynamic technological innovation at the end of the nineteenth century had been the opening of the world's first underground railway, which ran between Paddington and Farringdon Street. By the 1920s the original six-kilometre stretch of track had been extended to encompass vast areas of London and the suburbs, and escalators had been installed throughout the network to increase its accessibility to large numbers of passengers. It was truly one of the most potent symbols of the new industrial age, and one that Cyril Power seized upon eagerly (fig.16). All aspects of the Underground, from the old-fashioned spiral staircases that still led down to some of the platforms to the claustrophobic interiors of the trains themselves, fascinated him. The former, depicted in his 1929 linocut *The Tube Staircase* (fig.17), was inspired by the staircase at Russell Square station. It was discussed by the critic for *Apollo* in his review of the *First Exhibition of British Linocuts* at the Redfern.

Fig.14
Sybil Andrews
Concert Hall
1929
23.6 x 28 cm
9$\frac{1}{4}$ x 11 inches
Reproduced courtesy of the
Mary Ryan Gallery, New York

Fig.15
Sybil Andrews
Theatre
1929
27.5 x 20.5 cm
10⁷/₈ x 8 inches
Reproduced courtesy of the
Mary Ryan Gallery, New York

Fig.16
Cyril Power
The Tube Train
1934
31 x 31.5 cm
12 $\frac{1}{5}$ x 12 $\frac{1}{2}$ inches

Fig.17
Cyril Power
The Tube Staircase
1929
44.4 x 25.6 cm
17 1/2 x 10 inches

Fig.18
Cyril Power
Whence & Whither?
*c.*1930
31 x 24 cm
10 4/5 x 9 1/2 inches

'A good demonstration of the "trickiness" of this kind of design is Mr. Cyril Power's "Tube Staircase"; as one sees it, it is almost realistic and in that sense not quite right; turned upside down, it becomes immediately satisfying as a purely abstract rhythmic design.'[38] The more modern elements of the tube system were also recorded, *Whence & Whither?* (fig.18) depicting faceless commuters descending the escalators at Tottenham Court Road station as if travelling down to the fires of hell, the comparison given more strength by the fierce orange chosen for the walls of the tunnel. The remarkable technological advances that had allowed the construction of the tube were also included in Power's linocuts. *The Tube Station* of 1932 (fig.19) shows the curving tunnels, stretching into blackness and the hanging signs announcing the arrival of the next trains.

The first poster for London Underground Railways appeared in 1915 and under the guidance of Frank Pick, the head of publicity, every tube station and bus shelter was turned into a venue for constantly changing art exhibitions, aiming to show that every part of London was accessible through the newly amalgamated public transport system of buses, trams and tubes. Leading artists, such as Edward McKnight Kauffer, were commissioned to produce posters advertising sporting events, areas of the countryside and sights within London, which were then put on sale to the public in limited numbers, priced between two and five shillings, making them one of the cheapest forms of modern art available. Between 1929 and 1937 Sybil Andrews and Cyril Power were invited to produce seven designs for these placards and their work together, under the pseudonym 'Andrew-Power' resulted in a series of posters advertising sporting events which could be reached easily by public transport. The first of these promoted Southfields tube station, the alighting point for the Wimbledon tennis tournament, with others produced to cover cricket at Lord's and the Oval and ice hockey and skating at Wembley Park.

Fig.19
Cyril Power
The Tube Station
*c.*1932
25.8 x 29.5 cm
10¹/₈ x 11⁵/₈ inches

Fig.20
Andrew Power
Football
1933
Lithograph
101.6 x 63.5 cm
40 x 25 inches
Reproduced courtesy of
London's Transport Museum

Fig.21
Andrew Power
Epsom Summer Meeting
1933
Lithograph
101.6 x 63.5 cm
40 x 25 inches
Reproduced courtesy
of London's
Transport Museum

Fig.22
Sybil Andrews
Racing
1934
26 x 20.5 cm
10¼ x 8 inches

Perhaps the most famous of the designs was for Morden tube station at the southern end of the Northern line (fig.21). Crowds would disembark here and take a bus to Tattenham Corner in order to watch the annual Epsom Derby. The poster was based on Andrews' 1934 linocut, *Racing* (fig.22) which depicts the galloping field of horses coursing round Tattenham Corner in a dynamic flow of speed and colour.

Sport was a subject that fascinated both artists as it provided them with the opportunity to combine the fluidity of speed and dynamism with the expression of a release of physical effort. Some of Cyril Power's best-known works depict sportsmen and women in action, most notably his 1930 linocut, *The Eight* (fig.23) This print of a rowing eight was produced after Power had observed a team practising on the Thames from Hammersmith Bridge, which was not far from the studio he shared with Andrews. She too depicted the subject in her 1933, *Bringing in the Boat,* (fig.24) choosing instead to illustrate the aftermath when physical exertion was still required in order to return the boat to its house. Other activities depicted by Power include running (*The Runners, c.*1930 fig.25), skating (*Skaters, c.*1932 fig.26), tennis (*Tennis, c.*1933 fig.27) and dancing (*Divertissement, Folk Dance,* both *c.*1932 figs 28—9 and *Corps de Ballet, c.*1932 fig.30). While fewer of Andrews' linocuts concentrate on sport, she does appear to have had a particular fondness for activities that involved horses. Alongside her previously discussed image of *Racing*, she also concentrated on steeplechasing (*Steeplechasing,* 1930 and *Water Jump,* 1931, figs.31—2) and fox hunting (*In Full Cry,* 1931) although none of these works captured the velocity of the horses in such a striking way as her 1934 attempt at the subject.

Fig.23
Cyril Power
The Eight
1930
32.3 x 23.4 cm
12³/₄ x 9¹/₄ inches

Fig.24

Sybil Andrews

Bringing in the Boat

1933

33.2 x 26 cm

13 1/16 x 10 1/4 inches

Fig.25
Cyril Power
The Runners
*c.*1930
17.4 x 35 cm
6$^7/_8$ x 13$^3/_4$ inches

Fig.26
Cyril Power
Skaters
*c.*1932
19.8 x 31.6 cm
7 7/8 x 12 3/8 inches

The Futurists had picked one sport in particular as representative of the modern age. Motor racing had emerged at the turn of the century and quickly became a very popular pastime. While on the one hand it represented speed and danger, it also became a symbol of national pride, as countries battled with each other to produce the fastest cars and the most skilful drivers. Filippo Marinetti exclaimed in the manifesto of 1909 that introduced the Futurists, 'the world's magnificence has been enriched by a new beauty: the beauty of speed. A racing car whose hood is adorned with great pipes, live serpents of explosive breath — a roaring car that seems to ride on grapeshot is more beautiful than the *Victory of Samothrace.*'[39]

The Italian enthusiasm for motor sports was more than matched in England and the post-war period was characterised by the constant setting and breaking of record times by Malcolm Campbell, John Cobb and others in cars crafted by companies such as Napier, Bentley and Bugatti. The world's first purpose-built motor-racing circuit was constructed at Brooklands in Surrey and the races and endurance tests held there inspired Claude Flight's

Fig.27
Cyril Power
Tennis
*c.*1933
18.2 x 26.6 cm
7 1/8 x 10 1/2 inches

momentous linocut, *Brooklands* (fig.5), arguably the seminal work of the movement. His students were quick to absorb the motor-racing influence and both Cyril Power and Sybil Andrews produced linocuts on the theme. Power's 1932 *Speed Trial* (fig.34) was directly inspired by Malcolm Campbell's 'Bluebird', which first broke the land speed record at Pendine Sands in February 1927 and continued to set new times until 1935. The print is one of the clearest examples of the close links between the Grosvenor School artists and the early phase of Futurism as suggested by the pronounced airflow and aggressive force of the car.

Andrews also drew on the racing influence, most notably for her 1934 linocut, *Speedway* (fig.47), which depicts a motorbike trial. The idea was originally conceived for a London Transport Board poster earlier in the decade but never saw realisation. While Andrews certainly took an interest in the mechanisation of the modern world, her linocuts also looked back to the older, rural England, where work was accomplished through basic tools and physical exertion. Her 1932 print, *The Timber Jim* shows a team of horses straining on their harnesses to haul a log, the force of the effort apparent in the curved neck of the lead horse.

Fig.28
Cyril Power
Divertissement
*c.*1932
23.2 x 31.5 cm
9 1/8 x 12 1/2 inches

Manual labour is also present in Andrews' work; the
composition often centred on a single dominant focal point.
The Winch of 1930 (fig.35) clearly demonstrates this
technique, the two men striving together to turn the handle.
The print also appealed to contemporary critics, F. H. Hindle
writing that, '"The Winch" . . . is full of power, movement
and colour and the design of the two central figures is
amazingly simple and full of action'.[40] Similarly, her 1933
Sledgehammers (fig.36), a strong image of blacksmiths at
work, demonstrates the amount of physical activity that
was still required in the modern age.

Fig.29
Cyril Power
Folk Dance
*c.*1932
22 x 24.6 cm
8²/₃ x 9²/₃ inches

Fig.30
Cyril Power
Corps de Ballet
1932
28.2 x 28.2 cm
11 x 11 inches

Fig.31
Sybil Andrews
Steeplechasing
1930
17.5 x 27.2 cm
6⁷/₈ x 10³/₄ inches

Fig.32
Sybil Andrews
Water Jump
1931
31.2 x 21.3 cm
12^{1}/$_{4}$ x 8^{1}/$_{3}$ inches

Fig.33
William Greengrass
The First Fence
1932
23 x 28 cm
9 x 11 inches

An example of a more complicated linocut,
which utilises eight different lino-blocks

Fig.34
Cyril Power
Speed Trial
*c.*1932
19.6 x 37.5 cm
7 $^{3}/_{4}$ x 14 $^{3}/_{4}$ inches
Reproduced courtesy of the
Mary Ryan Gallery, New York

Fig.35
Sybil Andrews
The Winch
1930
18.4 x 28.4 cm
7 1/4 x 11 1/8 inches

Fig.36
Sybil Andrews
Sledgehammers
1933
26.4 x 31.6 cm
10 ³/₈ x 12 ³/₈ inches

Fig.37
Lill Tschudi
Sledging
1931
25.1 x 19.6 cm
$9^7/_8$ x $7^3/_4$ inches

Lill Tschudi

Of Flight's other pupils, the Swiss artist Lill Tschudi (1901–2001) was particularly close to her tutor despite only spending six months attending linocut classes. She enrolled at the Grosvenor in December 1929 after seeing an advertisement in *The Studio* magazine and studied with Flight until he left the school in May 1930. Between 1931 and 1933 Tschudi continued her studies in Paris, spending two months at the academy of the Cubist, Andre Lhote and also with the former Futurist, Gino Severini, and Fernand Leger at the Academie Ronson and the Academie Moderne respectively. Her subjects directly reflect those of Flight with their concentration on Futurist ideas of movement and rhythm. Her style is also closely related to his, including geometric designs and involving many of the key principles of Art Deco.

Tschudi too looked to sporting subjects for inspiration but her technique differed from the free-flowing forms that characterised the work of both Andrews and Power. Her *Sledging* of 1931 (fig.37) shows the solidity she applied to her figures but at the same time manages to capture the speed and dynamism of the downhill run. Similarly, her 1932 *In the Circus* (fig.38), depicting the arc of gymnasts swinging on the high bar, gives the human body a greater mass than either Andrews or Power had done. Nevertheless, the acrobats are still filled with vitality and movement. Tschudi was also very influenced by the time she spent in Paris and several of her linocuts depict the essence of European metropolitan life. Both *Sticking up Posters* (fig.39) and *Kiosk in Paris* (fig.40) of 1933 are typical of Parisian street scenes, the former in particular, showing the pasting of billposters outside a Metro station.

Fig.38
Lill Tschudi
In the Circus
1932
24 x 26 cm
9³/₈ x 10¹/₄ inches

Fig.39
Lill Tschudi
Sticking up Posters
1933
30.2 x 20 cm
11 $^7/_8$ x 7 $^7/_8$ inches
Reproduced courtesy of the
Mary Ryan Gallery, New York

Fig.40
Lill Tschudi
Kiosk in Paris
1933
22 x 26 cm
$8^2/_3$ x $10^1/_4$ inches

The Australians: Dorrit Black, Ethel Spowers and Eveline Syme

The school advertised in several publications, including *The Studio*, which has been credited as the greatest single influence on Australian printmaking before the 1940s. It was partly due to this advertising that Australian artists such as Dorrit Black, Eveline Syme and Ethel Spowers (1890–1947) joined the school during their 'grand tours' of Europe. These extended trips to Europe were becoming increasingly popular in Australia, especially among upper-middle-class women who were able to combine financial independence with society's gradual acceptance of their growing assertiveness. Dorrit Black left Sydney, alone, in 1927 and made her way directly to London, and to the Grosvenor School, having previously travelled around Europe with her family in 1910. Of the three artists, Black was the most inspired by her tutor and her prints reflect his interest in Art Deco design. She also shared many of his social ideals, having witnessed examples of extreme poverty during her time in Sydney. After she left the Grosvenor School she studied with Albert Gleizes and Frank Weitzel in Paris, whose influence is suggested by the Cubist elements in her work. The 1927–8 linocut, *Music* (fig.41) was inspired by an evening spent at the Dominium Art Club and reflects the vitality of the Jazz age in the vibrant dynamism of its background. Similarly, *The Acrobats* (fig.42) is conceived in the same style but employs a less severe abstraction in order to convey its message.

Arguably, Flight exerted less of a thematic influence on the other two Australian artists mentioned, Ethel Spowers and Eveline Syme. Instead, during their time at the Grosvenor School, both women learnt much technically from their tutor. Ethel Spowers favoured narrative images and was particularly fond of portraying children. However, her 1929–30 linocut *Wet Afternoon* (fig.43), with a range of umbrellas held high over heads in a London street, owes much to Flight's call to reflect modern life. Similarly *Special Edition* (fig.44) captures the frenetic and crowded quality of the city. Eveline Syme concentrated less on Flight's suggestions for subject matter but certainly explored some of his ideas concerning structure in linocuts. Works such as the 1929 *Skating* were clearly affected by his enthusiasm for geometric patterns.

Fig.41
Dorrit Black
Music
1927–8
24 x 21.4 cm
9 3/8 x 8 3/8 inches
National Gallery of Australia, Canberra
© Dorrit Black Estate

Fig.42
Dorrit Black
The Acrobats
1927–8
24 x 21.4 cm
9 3/8 x 8 3/8 inches
National Gallery of Australia, Canberra
© Dorrit Black Estate

Fig.43
Ethel Spowers
Wet Afternoon
1929–30
24.3 x 20.4 cm
9⅝ x 8⅛ inches
National Gallery of Australia, Canberra

Fig.44
Ethel Spowers
Special Edition
1936
28.2 x 22.6 cm
11 $^1/_{10}$ x 8 $^7/_8$ inches
National Gallery of Australia, Canberra

On the whole the critical reaction to the linocuts was favourable and the annual shows organised by Flight well received. The *First Exhibition of British Linocuts* was held in 1929 at the Redfern Gallery after Sir Rex Nan Kivell approached Flight on the recommendation of his co-director Knyvett Lee, who had attended one of the artist's lectures at the Grosvenor School. The shows ran at the Redfern until they transferred to the Ward Gallery on Baker Street in 1931, where they continued until 1937. Just as Marinetti had been the driving force behind Futurism, so Claude Flight actively promoted the linocut. Alongside the annual exhibitions, artists were encouraged to exhibit as often as possible as demonstrated by Cyril Power and Sybil Andrews' joint show at the Redfern in 1933 and Flight's solo exhibition at the Albany Gallery in 1931. Flight also worked to establish an international reputation for the School, touring the Redfern shows to Australia, China and America. In this aspect of promotion the linocuts were a success, George Bell writing in the *Sun* that the 1932 Redfern show in Melbourne was, 'an exhibition of great interest'.[41] He continued, 'the outstanding feature of the display is its vitality and creative force', noting that, 'women artists form the bulk of the good colour prints'.[42] Flight was delighted with the attention the exhibitions received; his joy was increased by the sales that were made during the shows. The *First Exhibition* in 1929 provoked great interest and over 100 prints were sold and Flight declared the show 'an outstanding success'.[43] Importantly, key collections such as the British Museum and the Victoria and Albert made purchases.

All three Australian artists played an important role in promoting both the School and the linocuts produced by its pupils abroad. Spowers in particular acted as an informal agent for Flight in Australia and ensured that several of his works were shown at the annual exhibition of the Arts and Crafts Society of Victoria. She also arranged shows devoted to linocut prints, the first being the 1930 *Exhibition of Linocuts* held in Melbourne. The shows did not immediately command critical acclaim, indeed Arthur Streeton writing in *The Argus*, expressed his disappointment with the medium. 'Judging from those shown so far in Melbourne designs printed from linoleum fall very far short in interest when compared with etchings and wood engravings.'[44] Despite this initial critical rejection, they soon gained acceptance, and the 1932 *Exhibition of Modern Colour Prints and Wood Engravings from the Redfern Gallery*, which toured to Melbourne received good reviews.

The linocuts of the Grosvenor School enjoyed a brilliant but all too brief popularity. By the mid-1930s the movement was losing direction and Claude Flight arranged the final exhibition as a retrospective at Birmingham City Museum and Art Gallery in 1939. By this time many of the key artists had gone their separate ways. Sybil Andrews left London in 1938 to move to Norley Wood in the New Forest while her working partner, Cyril Power, returned to his family in New Malden, Surrey. Lill Tschudi and the Australian artists had long since returned to their respective countries, and while many continued producing linocuts, the original momentum of the early years was lost. The public demand for art had also moved on and the linocuts were viewed as somewhat quaint relics of a past era. In the economic depression that preceded the Second World War the linocuts' bright optimism could only serve to strike a somewhat sour note and act as a reminder of better times.

Today the movement is once again prospering and public demand has never been so great. The revival began in November 1973 when Michael Parkin organised the first memorial exhibition of Claude Flight's work, eighteen years after his death. Parkin had been initially introduced to the designer Edith Lawrence through a mutual friend and he visited her at her home in Worth Matravers, Dorset with a view to exhibiting her work. Once there he was shown Flight's linocuts, all of which had been left to Lawrence

Fig.45
Cyril Power
The Merry-Go-Round
*c.*1930
30.5 x 30.4 cm
12 x 12 inches

following his death in 1955. The collection was immense, including twenty-seven copies of *Brooklands* alone and Parkin was able to produce a comprehensive exhibition, which charted the progress of Flight's œuvre. Following the successful show, Parkin travelled to the remote logging township of Campbell River on Vancouver Island, Canada where Sybil Andrews and her husband had lived since 1947. There he met the artist who was still producing linocuts and had several copies of her works of the 1920s and 1930s, despite losing many original blocks to the heat of the ship's hold during emigration. In 1975 Michael Parkin included Sybil Andrews' prints in his exhibition *Claude Flight and his Circle* and in 1980 he organised a solo exhibition of her work, *Sybil Andrews: Paintings and Graphic Work.*

In the early 1980s other galleries began to take an interest in the Grosvenor School linocuts, none more so than the Redfern on Cork Street where the early exhibitions had been held. Their first show, organised by Gordon Samuel in 1985 comprised of an overview of many of the School's pupils, including some lesser-known individuals such as Ronald Grierson and Leonard Beaumont. The work of Lill Tschudi in particular was taken up by the Coram Gallery, the predecessor of Scolar Fine Art, where an exhibition of her work, curated by Stephen Coppel, was held in 1995. While other shows concentrated solely on the linocuts produced during the 1920s and 1930s, the Coram exhibition also tracked the evolution of Tschudi's work in the years after she left the Grosvenor School, examining her continued use of the technique.

The new interest was not confined to England. The School's international appeal in the 1920s and 1930s ensured its popularity in countries such as Australia, Canada and America in the 1980s and 1990s. Sybil Andrews was quickly recognised in her adopted country and the Glenbow Museum of Calgary held an important exhibition of all her linocuts in 1982, producing a catalogue raisonné to accompany the show, which included a major essay by Peter White.

The exhibition toured Canada, further spreading Andrews' reputation. The linocuts also proved popular in Australia, both among the commercial and the public galleries. This interest was initially based in Melbourne, where many of the Australian artists connected with the School had organised exhibitions fifty years earlier, but it soon spread to Sydney and Canberra. Canberra proved to be of particular importance as it was home to the National Gallery of Australia where Stephen Coppel, now of the British Museum, took a special interest in the works. In 1995 Coppel published *Linocuts of the Machine Age: Claude Flight and the Grosvenor School*, the definitive work on the subject.

The enthusiasm for these linocuts remains undiminished. They exist as a reminder of a time when there was genuine excitement for the possibilities of the modern age and optimism for the future. They regularly achieve record prices at auction and there is a constant competition to acquire the more sought-after works. Certainly it is a far cry from Flight's initial aim of producing original art which could be purchased by the public for the price of a pint of beer.

Fig.46
Cyril Power
The Sunshine Roof
*c.*1934
26 x 33 cm
10 1/4 x 13 inches

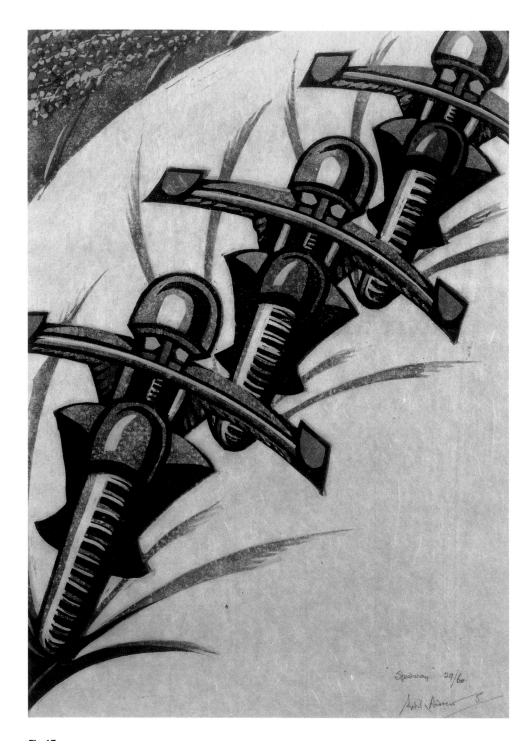

Fig.47
Sybil Andrews
Speedway
1934
32.6 x 23.3 cm
12^7/$_8$ x 9^1/$_8$ inches

Fig.48
Sybil Andrews
Football
1937
24.9 x 31.6 cm
9⁷/₈ x 12¹/₂ inches

References

1. The prospectus of the Grosvenor School of Modern Art was included in *This Year's Art 1935* compiled by A. C. R. Carter (London), 1935

2. P. G. Konody, 'The "7 & 5": Mr Claude Flight's Picture', *Observer*, no date, quoted in Lora S. Urbanelli, 'Claude Flight and the Grosvenor School of Modern Art: Origins, Development and Philosophy', *The Grosvenor School: British Linocuts Between the Wars*, p.14

3. W. Gaunt, 'The New Autumn Group', *The Studio*, 90, no.393 (December 1925), p.346

4. John Gould Fletcher, 'The Woodcut as Art', *Artwork*, 1, no.3 (February–April 1925), p.156

5. C. E. Dawson, 'Lino-Cuts. A New Method in Blockmaking for Posters and other Bold Work; also for making Tint-Blocks for Two-Color', *The Process Engraver's Monthly*, 14, no.157 (January 1907), p.16

6. Claude Flight, *The Art and Craft of Lino Cutting and Printing*, p.7

7. Frank Morley Fletcher quoted in Garton *et al.*, *British Printmakers 1855–1955*, p.238

8. Claude Flight quoted in Garton *et al.*, *British Printmakers 1855–1955*, p.238

9. Quoted in Coppel, *Linocuts of the Machine Age*, p.15

10. Eveline Syme speaking at the Arts and Crafts Society of Victoria, 1929, quoted in Coppel, *Linocuts of the Machine Age*, p.66

11. Claude Flight, *Lino-Cuts: A handbook of linoleum-cut colour printing*, pp.10–11

12. Ibid., p.9

13. Ibid., p.28

14. Ibid., p.34

15. Claude Flight, 'The Modern Colour-Print', *The Arts and Crafts Quarterly*, 1, no.2 (April 1925), p.6

16. See Coppel, *Linocuts of the Machine Age*, in which the printing techniques of each artist are discussed with regard to their individual linocuts

17. Sybil Andrews' letter to Lora S. Urbanelli (5 August 1986), quoted in Lora S. Urbanelli, 'Claude Flight and the Grosvenor School of Modern Art: Origins, Development and Philosophy', *The Grosvenor School: British Linocuts Between the Wars*, p.16

18. Claude Flight, *The Art and Craft of Lino Cutting and Printing*, p.63

19. Claude Flight, foreword, *Modern Colour Prints and Wood Engravings from the Redfern Gallery, London*, exh.cat., The Arts and Crafts Society of Victoria, Melbourne, 1932

20. Claude Flight, 'Linoleum-cut Colour Printing', *The Arts and Crafts Quarterly*, 1, no.6 (March 1926), p.6

21. Claude Flight, 'The Modern Colour-Print', *The Arts and Crafts Quarterly*, 1, no.2 (April 1925), p.7

22. Claude Flight, *Lino-Cuts: A handbook of linoleum-cut printing*, p.18

23. Ibid., p.46

24. Claude Flight, 'Linoleum-Cut Colour Printing', *The Arts and Crafts Quarterly*, 1, no.6 (March 1926), p.6

25. Claude Flight, *Lino-Cuts: A handbook of linoleum-cut colour printing*, notes for plate 9

26. Claude Flight, 'The Art of Today', *Colour*, 2, no.4 (April 1926), p.8

27. Maurice Fort, 'The Seven and Five Society', *Artwork*, 2, no.6 (January–March 1926), p.98

28. Letter from Claude Flight to Dorrit Black (25 March 1928), quoted in Ian North, *The Art of Dorrit Black*, p.22

29. Frank Rutter, 'Modern Painting', *Colour*, 1, no.1, 3rd Series (November 1928), p.3

30. Ibid., p.4

31. P. G. Konody, 'Speed in Art. Mr Flight's Dirt-Track Racers', *Daily Mail* (London), 8 November 1928, p.20

32. 'Mr. Claude Flight's Paintings at the Redfern Gallery', *Apollo*, 14, no.83 (November 1931), p.302

33. Sybil Andrews quoted in Gordon Samuel, 'Claude Flight and Associates: the British Linocut Movement', *British Colour Linocuts of the 1920s and 1930s*, exh.cat., Redfern Gallery, London, March–May 1985, p.7

34. Francis Carey and Anthony Griffiths, *Avant-garde British Printmaking 1914–1960*, p.84

35. Ibid., p.80

36. Coppel, *Linocuts of the Machine Age*, p.92

37. Claude Flight, 'Dynamism and the Colour Print', *The Original Colour Print Magazine*, vol.2, 1925, quoted in Coppel, 'Claude Flight and his followers: The colour linocut movement between the wars', catalogue essay for Australian touring exhibition (April 1992–July 1993), p.10

38. 'First Exhibition of British Linocuts at the Redfern Gallery', *Apollo*, 10, no.56 (August 1929), p.120

39. Filippo Marinetti, 'The Founding and Manifesto of Futurism', first published in *Le Figaro*, Paris, 20 February 1909

40. F. H. Hindle, 'Exhibition of Lino-Cuts. Examples of New Trends in Modern Art on Show at Shanghai Art Club', *The North-China Daily News* (Shanghai), 2 May 1931, p.14, quoted in Coppel, *Linocuts of the Machine Age*, p.107

41. George Bell, 'Colour Prints in Wide Range', *Sun*, 7 December 1932, p.15

42. Ibid.

43. Claude Flight, foreword, *Second Exhibition of Linocuts*, exh.cat., Redfern Gallery, London, 1930

44. A. Streeton, 'Linocuts', *The Argus* (Melbourne), 9 December 1930, p.5

Notes for Collectors

Literature

Undoubtedly the definitive work on the key artists of the Grosvenor School is Stephen Coppel's 1995 book, *Linocuts of the Machine Age*, published by Scolar Press in association with the National Gallery of Australia. Not only does this include a full catalogue raisonné of the work of Andrews, Black, Flight, Power, Spowers, Syme and Tschudi but it also contains essays on the life and art of the principal artists. We are constantly grateful to Stephen for his work in documenting the period so thoroughly.

Aside from *Linocuts of the Machine Age*, there are several other publications which throw additional light on the period and the artists, which are listed below.

Carey, Frances & Griffiths, Antony, *Avant-garde British Printmaking 1914–1960*, London, British Museum Publications, 1990

Flight, Claude, *Lino-Cuts: A Handbook of Linoleum-Cut Colour Printing*, Frome, Butler & Tanner Ltd, 1927; revised 1948

The Art of Lino-Cutting and Printing, London, B. T. Batsford, 1934

Garton, Robin *et al.*, *British Printmakers 1985–1955: A century of printmaking from the Etching Revival to St. Ives*, Aldershot, Garton & Co. in association with Scolar Press, 1992

Green, Oliver, *Underground Art: London Transport Posters 1908 to the Present*, London, Studio Vista, 1990

North, Ian, *The Art of Dorrit Black*, Melbourne, Art Gallery of South Australia and the Macmillan Co. of Australia Pty. Ltd, 1979

Samuel, Gordon, 'Claude Flight and Associates: The British Linocut Movement' in *British Colour Linocuts of the 1920s and 1930s by Sybil Andrews, Claude Flight & Cyril E. Power and the artists of the Grosvenor School of Modern Art*, exh.cat., Redfern Gallery, London, 1985

Samuel, Gordon and Gault, Richard 'The Linocut and the Grosvenor School of Modern Art: A Brief History' in *The Linocuts of Cyril Edward Power 1872–1951*, exh.cat., Redfern Gallery, London, 1989

Urbanelli, Lora S., 'Claude Flight and the Grosvenor School of Modern Art: Origins, Development and Philosophy' in *The Grosvenor School: British Linocuts between the Wars*, exh.cat., Rhode Island School of Design Museum of Art, Providence, 1988

White, Peter, 'Sybil Andrews' in *Sybil Andrews: Colour Linocuts: Linogravures en couleur*, exh.cat., Glenbow Museum, Calgary, 1982

While the principal artists of the Grosvenor School have already been discussed at length, Claude Flight had many other pupils who were eager to learn the technique of linocutting and in many cases produced outstanding examples of the medium. Several of these artists were included in the annual linocut exhibitions held at the Redfern and Ward galleries and received complimentary reviews in contemporary periodicals but for whatever reason are now more or less forgotten. While today the prints of Andrews, Flight, Power and the other key artists are scarce and regularly achieve record prices at auction, the linocuts of the lesser-known pupils are still available at prices that are conducive to building a collection. Below are some of the names to look for:

Beaumont, Leonard

Bissell, George

Boxius, S. G.

Bradshaw, Constance

Brien, Stanislavs

Burnett, R.

Carstairs, H.

Chart, D. D.

Collyer, Margaret

Drew, Diana

Edmonds, Paul

Falkner, A. L.

Finley, Anna R.

Fookes, Ursula

Greener, Leslie

Greengrass, William

Grierson, Ronald

Hardiman, A.

Harvey-Bloom, J.

Howey, R. L.

Kermode, William

Lockyer, I. de B.

McDowell, Mary

Mackenzie, E.

Malet, Guy W.

Mavrogordato, Julia

Mayo, Eileen

Meyer, Astrid

Mitchell, Enid B.

Nicholson, George

Paterson, Viola

Reyers, W.

Rowe, Hooper

Selby-Hall, R.

Sullivan, F.

Ward Hunt, O.

Weitzel, Frank

Wilson, R. A.

Wood, W. R.

Yonge, C. L.

Editions and Papers

Although Claude Flight did his very best to impress his own printing and editioning techniques on his pupils, many simply took them as a starting point from which they could experiment with their own methods. Significantly he was successful in convincing many of his students of the importance of order when printing, which resulted in several of the artists clearly numbering their editions in the fraction style with which we are familiar today. At the time this process was something of a novelty and artists would either leave their prints unnumbered or annotate them all with a phrase such as 'Artist's Proof'. The principal artists of the school also experimented with different papers, occasionally changing mid-edition. As discussed in the main essay, Flight often favoured the use of coloured backing papers, which would change the tonal scheme of the linocut. Again, Stephen Coppel has covered the various methods of the Grosvenor School artists in great detail so below is a brief summary:

Claude Flight

Editions of fifty declared but many prints were destroyed when Flight's studio at Rodmarton Mews was bombed during the Blitz.

Second editions of *Swingboats* and *Speed* were made for the American market, all of which are annotated 'USA'.

Flight experimented with various papers but preferred cream oriental laid tissue or thin oriental laid paper. He also used a thin grey laid paper and tracing paper for some impressions.

Cyril E. Power

1925–30 Editions of fifty (with some exceptions).

1931 onwards Editions of sixty.

Second edition of sixty of *The Tube Station* was made for the American market, annotated 'USA'.

Power occasionally only numbered the impression and did not state the edition size.

Proofs are annotated either 'EP' (Experimental Proof) or 'TP' (Trial Proof).

Most impressions are on tissue-like oriental paper.

Sybil Andrews

1929–30 Editions of fifty.

1931 onwards Editions of sixty (with a few exceptions).

Second editions of sixty of *Steeplechasing* and *Golgotha* were made for the American market, all of which are annotated 'USA'.

A third edition of sixty of *Steeplechasing* for the Australian market was started but only twenty prints were completed. These are annotated 'Aust'.

Proofs are labelled variously but Andrews certainly used the following annotations:

'EP' (Experimental Proof), 'TP' (Trial Proof), 'AP' (Artist's Proof), 'Specimen', 'AEP' (Artist's Experimental Proof), 'ATP' (Artist's Trial Proof) and 'AXP' (Artist's 'Extra' Proof).

Andrews generally used either oriental laid tissue or thin oriental laid paper for early impressions. After her move to Canada in 1947 she printed on thickish oriental paper, as her preferred thinner paper was not available.

Lill Tschudi

Editions of fifty.

Second editions of fifty of *Trio, In the Circus, Sailor's Holiday, Fixing the Wires, Ice Hockey, Concert II, Musicians* and *London Buses* were made for the American market, all of which are annotated 'USA'.

Early impressions were printed on either very delicate oriental laid tissue or oriental paper with laid lines. Later impressions were on soft, white mulberry paper.

Dorrit Black

Generally an edition of fifty was declared but very rarely completed.

Most impressions are printed on thin oriental laid paper or tissue.

Ethel Spowers

Usually editions of fifty.

Early prints were on thin oriental laid tissue with later impressions on buff oriental laid tissue.

Eveline Syme

Editions of twenty-five.

Mainly printed on buff oriental laid tissue.

Mounting and Displaying

Due to the printing methods employed by the linocut artists there is always a certain amount of extraneous ink in the margins of the prints, which was never intended to be seen by the owner. Many of the artists, Claude Flight in particular, marked the borders of the linocuts very clearly, with arrows, pencil lines and in some cases, brown tape. All of the images in this book have first been mounted to the correct margin before being photographed.

As with all prints, mounting and framing is best carried out by a professional framer who uses the correct, acid-free conservation materials. Linocuts should be hinge mounted with acid-free tape, not taped to a board with masking tape or worse, glued down; any form of self-adhesive tape should be avoided. Many linocuts that survive today have been damaged by the poor mounting and framing practices of previous years and it is not unusual to remove a print from its original 1930s board only to find that half the colours remain behind on the old acidic backing board.

The paper used by the Grosvenor School artists was superbly suited to its purpose and it has ensured that the linocuts we see today retain the same vibrant colours that were first produced in the 1920s and 1930s. In most cases the paper used was extremely thin, and while it has been proven sufficiently durable to last until now, it remains incredibly fragile. In particular, the prints can be damaged when their mounts are lifted, either by tearing or creasing.

Index of Works

List of works by principal artists as compiled by Stephen Coppel in *Linocuts of the Machine Age*, Scolar Press in association with the National Gallery of Australia, 1995

Reference numbers listed below correspond to Coppel's original ordering in *Linocuts of the Machine Age*.

Claude Flight (1881—1955)

Cyril E. Power (1872—1951)

Shadows, *c.*1926	CEP 5
Self-Portrait, 1927	CEP 6
Westminster Cathedral, Evening, *c.*1928	CEP 7
The Crypt, *c.*1928	CEP 8
(The High Altar, Westminster Cathedral), *c.*1928	CEP 9
The Carcase, *c.*1929	CEP 10
The Tube Staircase, 1929	CEP 11
The Escalator, *c.*1929	CEP 12
Lifts, *c.*1930	CEP 13
Whence & Whither?, *c.*1930	CEP 14
The Giant Racer, *c.*1930	CEP 15
The Merry-Go-Round, *c.*1930	CEP 16
En Grande Tenue or The Vestibule, *c.*1930	CEP 17
The Eight, 1930	CEP 18
The Runners, *c.*1930	CEP 19
Fire Dance, *c.*1931	CEP 20
Matriarchy, *c.*1931	CEP 21
Southampton-Le Havre, *c.*1931	CEP 22
Hockey, *c.*1931	CEP 23
Revolution, *c.*1931	CEP 24
The Vortex, *c.*1931	CEP 25
The Mummer, *c.*1931	CEP 26
Monseigneur St Thomas, 1931	CEP 27
Samson and the Lion, *c.*1932	CEP 28
Skaters, *c.*1932	CEP 29
Folk Dance, *c.*1932	CEP 30
Speed Trial, *c.*1932	CEP 31
The Tube Station, *c.*1932	CEP 32
Divertissement, *c.*1932	CEP 33
Corps de Ballet, 1932	CEP 34
Acrobats, *c.*1933	CEP 35
'Appy 'Ampstead, *c.*1933	CEP 36
The High Swing, *c.*1933	CEP 37
Tennis, *c.*1933	CEP 38
The Sunshine Roof, *c.*1934	CEP 39
The Exam Room, *c.*1934	CEP 40
The Tube Train, *c.*1934	CEP 41
Air Raid, *c.*1935	CEP 42
The Concerto, *c.*1935	CEP 43
The Trio, *c.*1936	CEP 44
St Francis, *c.*1937	CEP 45

Sybil Andrews (1898–1992)

Concert Hall, 1929	SA 1
Theatre, 1929	SA 2
Oranges, 1929	SA 3
Haulers, 1929	SA 4
Straphangers, 1929	SA 5
The Winch, 1930	SA 6
Bathers, 1930	SA 7
Wet Race Meeting, 1930	SA 8
Rush Hour, 1930	SA 9
Steeplechasing, 1930	SA 10
The Gale, 1930	SA 11
Pas Seul or Sculls, 1930	SA 12
In Full Cry, 1931	SA 13
Water Jump, 1931	SA 14
Golgotha, 1931	SA 15
Hyde Park, 1931	SA 16
The Giant Cable *or* The New Cable, 1931	SA 17
The Captive, 1932	SA 18
Deposition, 1932	SA 19
Joseph and Nicodemus, 1932	SA 20
The Timber Jim, 1932	SA 21
Mother and Son, 1932	SA 22
Pietà, 1932	SA 23
Bringing in the Boat, 1933	SA 24
Otter Hunt, 1933	SA 25
Sledgehammers, 1933	SA 26
The Windmill, 1933	SA 27
Flower Girls, 1934	SA 28
Speedway, 1934	SA 29
Fall of the Leaf, 1934	SA 30
Tillers of the Soil, 1934	SA 31
Racing, 1934	SA 32
Michaelmas, 1935	SA 33
Storm, 1935	SA 34
Via Dolorosa, 1935	SA 35
Tumulus, 1936	SA 36
Haysel, 1936	SA 37
Market Day, 1936	SA 38
Mowers, 1937	SA 39
Football, 1937	SA 40
Swans, 1939	SA 41
Prodigal Son, 1939	SA 42
Gipsies, 1939	SA 43
Jesus Bears the Cross: Station II, 1946	SA 44
Joseph of Arimathea: Station XIII, 1946	SA 45

Gethsemane, 1951	SA 46	Prof. Dr Ramel, 1930	LT 13
In Manus Tuas Domini: Station XII, 1951	SA 47	The Flirt, 1930	LT 14
Indian Dance, 1951	SA 48	Lime Kiln, 1931	LT 15
Logging Team, 1952	SA 49	*Hors Concours*, 1931	LT 16
Hauling, 1952	SA 50	Sledging, 1931	LT 17
Coffee Bar, 1952	SA 51	National Vote I, 1931	LT 18
Skaters, 1953	SA 52	Song of the Volga Boatmen, 1931	LT 19
Pilate: Station I, 1953	SA 53	Gymnastic Exercises, 1931	LT 20
Ploughing Pasture, 1955	SA 54	Mountain Valley, 1931	LT 21
Tenebrae: Station XIV, 1956	SA 55	Trio, 1931	LT 22
Mangolds, 1956	SA 56	In the Circus, 1932	LT 23
Surrexit, 1957	SA 57	Sailors' Holiday, 1932	LT 24
Grader, 1959	SA 58	*Affaire d'Honneur*, 1932	LT 25
Rock, 1960	SA 59	Fixing the Wires, 1932	LT 26
Sails, 1960	SA 60	Haymaking, 1932	LT 27
Trackway *or* Piste, 1961	SA 61	Just Off *or* The Start of the Race, 1932	LT 28
Day's End, 1961	SA 62	Kiosk in Paris, 1933	LT 29
Plough, 1961	SA 63	Nudes, 1933	LT 30
Jesus Falls the First Time: Station III, 1962	SA 64	Ice Hockey, 1933	LT 31
Peevies, 1962	SA 65	Corporal of the Infantry, 1933	LT 32
Father Forgive Them: Station XI, 1964	SA 66	Sticking up Posters, 1933	LT 33
Jesus Meets His Mother: Station IV, 1964	SA 67	The Skier, 1933	LT 34
Peter, 1966	SA 68	Skiing, 1934	LT 35
Anno Domini, 1970	SA 69	Chinese Jugglers, 1934	LT 36
Dance of the Birds, 1975	SA 70	Cleaning a Sail, 1934	LT 37
Tracks, 1977	SA 71	*Jeu de Boules*, 1934	LT 38
Jesus Falls the Second Time: Station VII, 1977	SA 72	The Helmsman, 1934	LT 39
Jesus Falls for the Third Time: Station IX, 1978	SA 73	Village Fair I, 1934	LT 40
Wings, 1979	SA 74	Ski Weekend, 1935	LT 41
Fleece, 1985	SA 75	French Porters, 1935	LT 42
Six Waterpots of Stone, 1988	SA 76	*Tour de Suisse*, 1935	LT 43
		Rumba Band I, 1935	LT 44
		Jazz Orchestra, 1935	LT 45
Lill Tschudi (1911–2001)		Pierrot, 1935	LT 46
Race in Switzerland, 1930	LT 1	Waiters, 1936	LT 47
Sailors, 1930	LT 2	Rumba Band II, 1936	LT 48
Saphis, 1930	LT 3	Carnival, 1936	LT 49
Underground, 1930	LT 4	Guards, 1936	LT 50
Sword Drill, 1930	LT 5	Stepdancing, 1936	LT 51
Jazz Band, 1930	LT 6	Furniture Removal I, 1936	LT 52
Difficult Parking, 1930	LT 7	Visiting Day, 1937	LT 53
Telescope, 1930	LT 8	Ski-Joring, 1937	LT 54
The Broken Window: Portrait of Clive Brook, 1930	LT 9	Dancers, 1937	LT 55
Clive Brook, 1930	LT 10	Workmen, 1937	LT 56
Foxtrot, 1930	LT 11	Street Decoration, 1937	LT 57
Sunday Morning *or* Bear-pit, 1930	LT 12	Bells, 1937	LT 58

Eveline Syme (1888–1961)

Index